# BOOK OF CURIOUS BIRDS

## JENNIFER COSSINS

LOTHIAN
Children's Books

For Tess, with so much love x

A Lothian Children's Book

Published in Australia and New Zealand in 2021
by Hachette Australia
Level 17, 207 Kent Street, Sydney NSW 2000
www.hachettechildrens.com.au

Text and illustrations copyright © Jennifer Cossins 2021

NATIONAL
LIBRARY
OF AUSTRALIA

A catalogue record for this
book is available from the
National Library of Australia

ISBN 978 0 7344 2047 3 (hardback)

Designed by Kinart
Colour reproduction by Splitting Image
Printed in China by Toppan Leefung Printing Limited

# CONTENTS

Introduction

Southern cassowary   2

Ribbon-tailed astrapia   4

Kagu   6

Secretary bird   8

Rhinoceros hornbill   10

Sword-billed hummingbird   12

Palm cockatoo   14

Guianan cock-of-the-rock   16

Philippine eagle   18

Capuchinbird   20

Blue-footed booby   22

Twelve-wired bird-of-paradise   24

Shoebill   26

Hoatzin   28

North Island brown kiwi   30

Hooded pitohui   32

Ocellated turkey   34

Tawny frogmouth   36

Vogelkop superb bird-of-paradise   38

Tufted coquette   40

Greater sage-grouse   42

Tufted puffin   44

Great grey owl   46

Greater prairie-chicken   48

Magnificent frigatebird   50

White-headed duck   52

Vulturine guinea fowl   54

Wandering albatross   56

Glossary   58

Acknowledgements

About the author

# INTRODUCTION

Birds are curious creatures. Some are dazzlingly beautiful and others just plain weird looking. Some are common; others are endangered and need our protection to survive. Some are so shy they are rarely seen and little is known about them, while others show no fear of humans and can recognise individual faces. Some are sneaky, some are artistic, some make and use tools, some can learn to talk and some are even poisonous!

I wrote this book because I've long been fascinated by the numerous strange birds in our world. Birds are my favourite animals to draw and I am thrilled to be able to dedicate a whole book to drawing such remarkable creatures. As an artist, I am attracted to the most unusual looking birds – the ugly ones as well as the bizarrely beautiful. But beyond their looks, I wanted to find out which birds are the biggest, which fly the fastest, which ones have the longest feathers, the longest beak, the longest legs. I knew of several birds I wanted to include, but the process of researching led me down many new paths and so I have included a few I hadn't even heard of before.

In this book you'll find colourful feathers alongside peculiar beaks, beady eyes and funny-coloured feet. You'll read of dangerous birds, clever birds, fast birds, awkward birds, silly birds, massive birds and tiny birds. You'll laugh at their odd hairdos, marvel at their remarkable hunting skills and admire their wild mating dances. Most of all, you'll learn that birds are awesome and deserve our love, care and respect.

This is a book for bird lovers. If you are not one already, I hope that after reading this you'll join me in my love of curious birds.

# SOUTHERN CASSOWARY

## The most dangerous bird alive

**Location:** Tropical forests and wetlands of northern Australia

**Lifespan:** 19 years

**Height:** 1.5–2 m

**Conservation status:** Endangered

There are three species of cassowary and the southern cassowary is the largest, making it the second heaviest bird in the world after the ostrich.

Cassowaries are flightless and one of the closest living species to dinosaurs, with a serious reputation as the world's most dangerous bird. They are reclusive and shy, but become territorial when threatened — especially the females, which are larger, more brightly coloured and more aggressive than the males. The kick of a cassowary is what makes it so dangerous. Each foot has a dagger-like middle claw that can grow up to ten centimetres long and can slice open a potential predator with one swift kick. Cassowaries are also excellent swimmers and fast runners, their powerful legs helping them run at 50 kilometres an hour and jump two metres in the air.

Cassowaries communicate using many sounds — they hiss, whistle, clap their bills and make a deep, rumbling boom that is the lowest known call of any living bird. The call is so low that it can barely be heard by humans.

Cassowaries are generally solitary creatures, only coming together to breed. Once she lays her eggs, the female cassowary leaves and it is the male who incubates them. He stays with the eggs for 50 days, rarely eating or drinking. After they hatch, the male raises the chicks until they are almost fully grown, at around ten months old.

# RIBBON-TAILED ASTRAPIA

## The ribbon twirler

**Location:** Central highlands of Papua New Guinea
**Weight:** 102–165 g

**Length:** 30–35 cm (not including the male's tail)
**Conservation status:** Near threatened

The ribbon-tailed astrapia is one of the most spectacular birds-of-paradise, named after the males' long white tail feathers.

They have some of the longest tail feathers, in relation to body size, in the bird kingdom — the feathers can be over a metre long!

Given their bodies are only about 30 centimetres in length, the males' feathers create a truly dramatic appearance. These feathers can cause problems, though. They sometimes get tangled up in the dense rainforest foliage while the male is foraging, and can slow him down if a predator is near and he needs to make a quick escape.

During mating season, male ribbon-tailed astrapias come together to perform a communal courtship display for the females. Gatherings for communal displays are practised by a number of bird species and are known as leks. Male ribbon-tailed astrapias' displays usually involve lots of jumping between branches with their long tail feathers arched up behind and over their heads, ready to swish around dramatically to attract a female.

Ribbon-tailed astrapia males are polygynous — they mate with several different females each breeding season. The females alone build and tend to the nests and raise the chicks, returning to the same place to build their nest each season.

# KAGU

## The ghost of the forest

**Location:** Forests of New Caledonia

**Wingspan:** About 80 cm

**Length:** 55 cm

**Conservation status:** Endangered

The kagu is only found in the mountain forests of New Caledonia. It is endemic to that specific area because it can't be found anywhere else in the world. Unlike other forest birds that are dark and mottled to help them camouflage, kagus stand out with their bright white and light grey feathers.

Although flightless, kagus have full-sized wings that they use to glide when escaping danger. These wings are also an important part of their distinctive displays. Underneath a kagu's wings are dramatic black and white striped feathers, which they show off both in courtship and in territorial disputes. On these occasions, kagus will also erect their long crests and strut around each other in a slow circle.

## The kagu is the only bird that has nasal corns — small structures covering its nostrils.

It is thought these corns evolved to protect their nostrils from dust and dirt, as kagus spend so much time rooting around on the forest floor for food. Kagus are carnivorous — most birds eat a combination of insects and plant matter, but kagus are meat eaters only, with their favourite foods being worms, snails, lizards and spiders.

Kagus are monogamous (meaning they have only one mate) and form long-term pairs. While they tend to forage alone during the day, mated pairs begin each morning with a unique 15-minute duet. The male and female sound distinctly different and the song, which can be heard up to two kilometres away, has been likened to the sound of a barking puppy. Kagu parents share responsibility for incubating their single egg, taking turns every 24 hours.

# SECRETARY BIRD

## The snake hunter

**Location:** Savannah of sub-Saharan Africa

**Wingspan:** 2.1 m

**Height:** 1.2–1.5 m

**Conservation status:** Endangered

No one really knows how these African birds got their strange name, and that's not the only curious thing about them.

Secretary birds have the longest legs of all raptors (birds of prey). They are one of only two raptors that hunt on the ground instead of in the air, spending most of their time strolling through the savannah and grasslands of southern Africa. Despite their preference for land, they can fly extremely well, soaring through the sky and trailing their long legs behind them.

Secretary birds eat rodents, frogs and insects, but they have a fierce reputation as snake killers. Their impulse to kill snakes is so strong they will attack anything that looks like a snake, even an inanimate object.

When attacking, secretary birds will raise their wings and head feathers, then strike with their hooked beaks or stomp with their claws until their prey is either dead or stunned enough to swallow whole!

Secretary birds are monogamous and lay their eggs in large nests high up in acacia trees. They are usually quiet birds, but if a predator is threatening the nestlings the parent birds will make low croaks or roaring groans to scare it off.

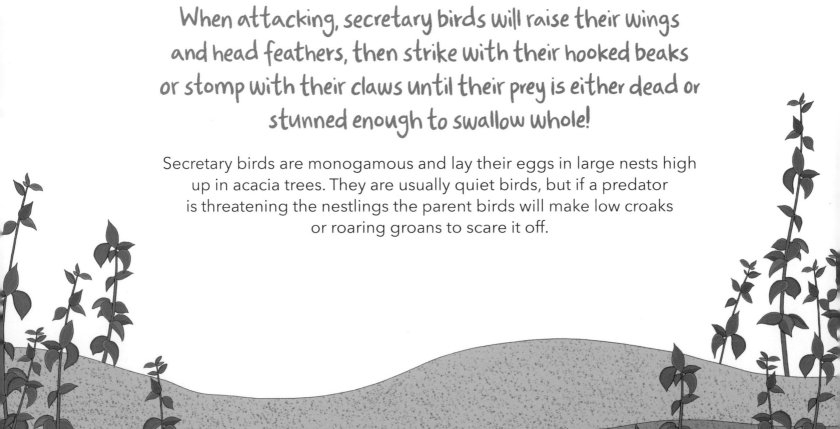

# RHINOCEROS HORNBILL

## The rhino of the trees

**Location:** Tropical forests of Indonesia and Malaysia

**Wingspan:** 1.5–1.8 m

**Length:** 80–120 cm

**Conservation status:** Vulnerable

This striking tropical bird has a helmet-like feature on its head called a casque. It is one of the largest casques in the world and its unique shape is where this particular hornbill gets its name. The casque is made of keratin (the same stuff your fingernails are made from) and is hollow inside. It is thought that this creates a resonating chamber, amplifying the calls of the rhinoceros hornbill and helping its calls travel further in the forest.

When rhinoceros hornbill chicks are born their beaks and casques are white, and it is not until around six years of age that they change colour.

## The bright orange of their casques comes from preen oil, which the birds rub on from a gland above their tails while they preen — tidying and cleaning their feathers.

Male and female rhinoceros hornbills look similar, but the females are larger and have white eyes, while the males have red eyes.

Rhinoceros hornbills mate for life and the bond between pairs is important, as the female stays with the eggs, then the chicks, while the male brings them food. After building a nest inside a tree trunk and laying the eggs, the pair block the entrance to the nest with mud, leaving a tiny hole just big enough for the male to pass in food for his family.

The female usually has one to two chicks. Once the chicks are about a month old, she leaves the nest — resealing it behind her but leaving a hole to feed them through — until they are ready to leave the nest as well.

# SWORD-BILLED HUMMINGBIRD

## The little sword-wielder

**Location:** Tropical forests of the Andes Mountains, South America

**Weight:** 10–15 g

**Length:** 14 cm (not including the beak)

**Conservation status:** Least concern

The sword-billed hummingbird is tiny with a very long beak. Their beaks are around eight to ten centimetres long, making them the only bird with a longer beak than body (not including the tail).

Such a long beak and tongue allows this bird to reach nectar that other birds, butterflies and bees cannot, making the sword-billed hummingbird an extremely important pollinator. It is the only bird that can reach the nectar deep inside the long, tubular *Passiflora mixta*, so this flower relies on the sword-billed hummingbird alone to pollinate and survive.

The sword-billed hummingbird is one of the only birds that uses its feet to preen itself, as its enormous beak is too long to reach its own feathers.

Like other hummingbirds, sword-billed hummingbirds can remember every flower they have visited. Their large brains help their memory – hummingbirds have the largest brain of any bird in proportion to their body size, making up about 4.2 per cent of their body weight. Our human brain is only 2 per cent of our body weight!

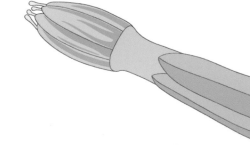

# PALM COCKATOO

## The drumming parrot

**Location:** Rainforests of New Guinea and northern Australia

**Wingspan:** 70-100 cm

**Length:** 55-60 cm

**Conservation status:** Least concern

Palm cockatoos are the largest parrots. They live in regions with heavy rainfall and are often seen hanging upside down in the rain, stretching out their wings and tails for a bath.

## They have red cheeks that can flush deep scarlet when they are stressed or excited.

Palm cockatoos have unique beaks. They are not only the second largest beak of any parrot, but the shape of them means they never close completely. This allows the cockatoo to hold a nut in its beak and crack it at the same time.

Palm cockatoos are one of very few bird species known to use tools. To stake out his territory, the male breaks off a small tree branch with his beak and, holding the branch in one foot, beats it repeatedly against a hollow tree. This drumming can be heard up to 100 metres away. Afterwards, the male often strips his drumstick into small pieces and gets to work using it to build a nest in the chosen tree.

Palm cockatoos mate for life and the females lay only one egg every two years. This is one of the slowest breeding rates of any bird. Chicks are looked after by both parents and leave the nest, or fledge, in about three months, which is the longest fledging time of any parrot.

# GUIANAN COCK-OF-THE-ROCK

## The orange rocker

**Location:** Rocky gorges of the Andes Mountains, South America
**Weight:** 200–220 g

**Height:** About 30 cm
**Conservation status:** Least concern

These fancy-feathered birds get their name from the way they nest under rocky overhangs, on cliff faces or in caves. They mostly feed on fruit and insects but occasionally enjoy a small lizard or frog as well.

Male and female Guianan cock-of-the-rocks look very different — the females are mostly brown, while the males sport the frilly orange plumage these birds are known for.

The males use their feathers in their dramatic leks. As many as 50 males gather for the courtship display, each one claiming a space on the forest floor for his performance. They then compete, jumping, flapping, glaring, snapping their beaks and squawking raucously. When one of the watching females flies in to look more closely, the males wait, silent and still, with all their feathers fluffed up and spread out to show off their magnificent colours, trying to appear as irresistible as possible. If a female likes what she sees, she will fly down and choose her mate by pecking him on the rump or neck.

After mating, all the work is left to the female, who has already built a nest of mud and plant material, bound together with her saliva. She lays one to two eggs in her nest, incubates them and raises the chicks by herself. The chicks leave the nest after about 44 days.

# PHILIPPINE EAGLE

## The blue-eyed monkey-eater

**Location:** Four islands of the Philippines

**Wingspan:** 1.9 m on average

**Height:** Around 1 m

**Conservation status:** Critically endangered

Philippine eagles are incredibly rare and endemic to only four of the 7000-plus islands that make up the Philippines. They are among the most powerful birds in the world, and are able to fly at speeds of up to 100 kilometres an hour!

### Philippine eagles are the only raptors with blue eyes.

Their eyes are incredibly powerful, too — they can see about eight times further than humans, which helps them hunt in the dense Philippine forests. They were first named monkey-eating eagles because it was believed they ate only monkeys, but these carnivorous birds are not fussy. They will hunt flying squirrels, bats, snakes, civets, other birds of prey and even domestic animals like dogs and pigs.

Philippine eagles are monogamous and, once paired, they stay together for the rest of their lives. Pairs have been seen working together to hunt, with one eagle distracting the prey while the other swoops in from behind.

Mated pairs are devoted parents and build huge nests together that they use year after year for their young. The female lays one egg every two years, and the chick, called an eaglet, is nurtured by both parents for around 20 months.

# CAPUCHINBIRD

## The bald monk of the jungle

**Location:** Tropical lowland forests of north-eastern South America
**Weight:** Around 340–420 g

**Length:** Around 35 cm
**Conservation status:** Least concern

The capuchinbird's name comes from its 'hood' of neck feathers that make this bird look a little like it's wearing the robes of a Capuchin monk. Their heads appear much too small for their bodies because they are featherless. Adding to their unusual appearance is the male's fluffy orange under-tail feathers, which are only really visible during mating displays.

Male and female capuchinbirds look mostly alike, and both are solitary creatures until breeding season begins and they gather in leks. A capuchinbird lek is a bizarre sight to see. The male birds, led by a dominant male, sit on a perch and stretch upright with their feathers extended.

### They make a deep call, which sounds like a cross between a mooing cow and a distant chainsaw.

Female capuchinbirds are attracted by the sound and come to see the lek. The dominant male must continually defend his perch from the other males who long for a shot at the top of the pecking order. Meanwhile, the females become quite aggressive towards each other as they try to move as close as possible to the dominant male. With the males and females each fighting among themselves, the lek quickly becomes chaotic. It is usually only the dominant male that gets to mate with multiple females, so the competition is fierce!

# BLUE-FOOTED BOOBY

## The clown of the Galapagos

**Location:** Galapagos Islands and western coast of Central and South America

**Wingspan:** 1.5 m

**Length:** 80 cm

**Conservation status:** Least concern

The blue-footed booby is a marine bird famous for its humorous waddle, piercing yellow eyes and bright blue feet. Females are slightly bigger than males and have deeper blue feet. Another way to tell males and females apart is their eyes – males have more yellow eyes with small pupils, whereas females have much larger, star-shaped pupils.

The name 'booby' comes from the Spanish word *bobo*, meaning foolish, which was perhaps unfairly applied to these remarkable birds because of their clumsy movement on land, and the fact they are unafraid of people and easily caught.

Boobies have a peculiar way of cooling themselves down: they open their mouths and flutter the skin of their necks, which makes them appear to be laughing.

Boobies spend most of their lives at sea and are expert divers. They breathe through their beaks because their nostrils are permanently sealed to stop water going in as they dive-bomb fish at speeds of up to 100 kilometres an hour. They even have a special air sac in their skulls to protect their heads from the impact of hitting the water so fast.

During the breeding season, blue-footed boobies perform a comical courtship dance, with the males strutting and stomping around to show off their feet to the females. The brighter blue the feet, the more attractive they are to females. Once paired up, they circle each other, whistling, honking and marching together.

# TWELVE-WIRED BIRD-OF-PARADISE

## The wiry dancer

**Location:** Lowland rainforests of Papua New Guinea and Indonesia

**Weight:** Around 170–220 g

**Length:** 33–35 cm

**Conservation status:** Least concern

The stunning twelve-wired bird-of-paradise feeds on fruit, insects and nectar. They are very territorial, with each male trying to stay at least 700 metres away from any other male in the region.

Male and female twelve-wired birds-of-paradise look very different from each other, with females slightly larger than the males. It takes the males about seven years to fully develop their striking yellow and black feathers, while the females much more easily blend into their environment with brown, black and white feathers.

## Only the males have 'wires', exactly six on each side of their tail feathers, which bend up at strange angles.

These birds have a dynamic courtship dance. While other male birds-of-paradise choose horizontal branches to perform on, the male of this species chooses a vertical branch. He uses his twelve wires for a specific dance move, known as the 'wire-wipe display', where he shows off by swishing the wires in the female's face. But this doesn't always go to plan. The wires can get caught in the female's beak and the male often appears so focused on his performance that he doesn't even notice, continuing to dance while the female struggles to remove the wires from her beak.

# SHOEBILL

## The giant-billed stork

**Location:** Swamps and wetlands of Central and East Africa

**Wingspan:** 2.3 m

**Height:** 1–1.5 m

**Conservation status:** Vulnerable

At over a metre tall, with an even wider wingspan, shoebills are a formidable presence in the wetlands they call home. They often stand motionless for hours with their giant bills held down against their necks, staring out at the world with beady eyes. When they fly, they have one of the slowest flap rates of any bird.

Lungfish are the shoebill's favourite food, but they will also eat catfish, eels, lizards, snakes and even baby crocodiles. Shoebills have an unusual hunting method – they stand completely still in the water for hours on end until an unsuspecting creature comes along. Then they collapse on top of them with incredible force, wings spread and their bills open wide, devouring the creature whole.

## Shoebills have a habit of pooing on their own legs to cool themselves down when it's too hot — a trait they share with many other storks that live in hot climates.

Most of the time shoebills are quiet, but when mating season comes around they can be very noisy, making a series of popping sounds with their bills similar to a machine gun. Potential mates love this unusual sound!

Shoebills form monogamous pairs but as solitary creatures they rarely spend time together unless it's breeding season. The female usually lays two eggs and both parents tend to them, turning them regularly and keeping them cool by filling their large bills with water and pouring it over the eggs.

# HOATZIN

## The flying cow

**Location:** Swamps, marshes and riverbanks of northern South America

**Weight:** Up to 900 g

**Length:** 61-66 cm

**Conservation status:** Least concern

The hoatzin is known by many names, including stink bird or skunk bird because of its notoriously stinky odour, and reptile bird because of its unusual featherless head.

## Hoatzins are the only birds that primarily eat leaves and as such they have a unique digestive system.

Like cows, their stomachs use bacterial fermentation to break down their food, which causes these birds to smell quite bad. This special digestive system is large and takes up so much room in their bodies that their flight muscles and sternum are much smaller than most birds, making them clumsy and poor fliers.

Another strange feature of the hoatzin is that the chicks are born with tiny claws on the front of their wings which they lose as they grow into adulthood. No one knows why these claws exist, but they do come in handy – hoatzins nest in tree branches that overhang water, and if a chick finds itself in danger, it simply jumps out of the nest into the water, before swimming back to shore and using its wing claws to climb out of the water, up the tree and back into the nest.

# NORTH ISLAND BROWN KIWI

## The whiskered wonder

**Location:** New Zealand's North Island

**Lifespan:** 25-50 years

**Height:** 50-65 cm

**Conservation status:** Vulnerable

The North Island brown kiwi is the largest and most common of New Zealand's five species of kiwi.

## While their closest relatives are emus and cassowaries, kiwis have many features that are more like mammals.

They have unusually heavy bones for a bird and muscular legs that enable them to outrun humans. They also have a much more highly developed sense of smell than most birds and they are the only bird with nostrils at the end of their beaks. Their tiny flightless wings, only a few centimetres long, hide under their unusually shaggy feathers that look more like fur. They even have whiskers!

Female kiwis lay huge eggs. They have one of the largest egg-to-body ratios of any bird, with eggs that are 15 to 20 per cent of their body weight. The male kiwi incubates the eggs for about 80 days, which is more than twice the average time for most birds and more like the gestation time of a small mammal. Kiwi chicks then kick open their shells fully feathered and independent, looking like miniature versions of their parents. They don't need to be fed as they are born with special yolk sacs attached to their bellies which sustain them for the first ten days of their lives until they can forage for their own food.

# HOODED PITOHUI
## The deadly songbird

**Location:** Tropical rainforests of New Guinea
**Weight:** About 65 g

**Length:** About 23 cm
**Conservation status:** Least concern

There are very few poisonous birds in nature and the brightly coloured songbird known as the hooded pitohui is the most toxic of them all. With their bright orange plumage and unpleasant smell, hooded pitohuis are a good example of aposematism, which is when animals use colour, pattern or smell as a warning sign to tell others they are toxic or dangerous.

Hooded pitohuis eat mostly fruit and seeds, but they also eat the *Choresine* beetle, which is where they get their poison from. The poison, called homobatrachotoxin, is found in their feathers and skin.

## Touching them will cause numbness and tingling and, in high enough doses, paralysis and death.

Hooded pitohuis lay their eggs in cup-shaped nests made from vines. The female rubs poison from her feathers onto the eggs while incubating them. This makes the eggs very unappealing to predators passing by when the female has left the nest for food. In fact, snakes have been observed swallowing the eggs whole, then vomiting them back up again after they detect the poison. An impressive defence mechanism for a small bird!

# OCELLATED TURKEY

## The strutting rainbow

**Location:** Central America, usually forested areas
**Weight:** 3–4.5 kg

**Length:** 70–100 cm (including tail)
**Conservation status:** Near threatened

The ocellated turkey is a spectacular bird that is endemic to a few small forested regions of Mexico, Belize and Guatemala. While they are good flyers, they prefer to spend most of their time on the ground, scratching around for their food, which includes insects, fruits, grass seeds and leaves. They settle to sleep or rest (known as roosting) in trees to stay safe from wild cats like jaguars, margays and ocelots.

Famous for their metallic, rainbow-coloured feathers that appear to shimmer in the sun, ocellated turkeys have featherless heads with many wart-like bumps.

### Their special bumps can vary in colour according to mood, becoming brighter and bolder — especially during mating season.

Males and females look similar, but males have brighter colours and are larger than the females. Males also have a spur on the back of their legs that grows longer as they age, averaging around four centimetres long.

Male ocellated turkeys perform complex mating dances to impress females, involving lots of crouching, foot-stamping, strutting and tail waving, often all while vibrating their wings and fanning out their magnificent tail feathers.

The name 'ocellated' comes from the Latin word *ocellus*, meaning 'eye', after their eye-like tail feather markings.

# TAWNY FROGMOUTH

## The ultimate master of disguise

**Location:** Throughout Australia
**Wingspan:** 64-97 cm

**Height:** 20-53 cm
**Conservation status:**
Least concern

Tawny frogmouths are very hard birds to spot. During the day they roost in trees, their feathers camouflaging them as they hide from predators. If they sense danger, they will freeze with their heads raised and their eyes closed. This is known as 'stumping' because it makes them appear like a broken tree branch.

Commonly known as 'tawnies', the name 'frogmouth' comes from their unusually wide mouths that look like a frog's mouth.

Tawnies are noisy birds. When they are annoyed they sound like they are laughing, and when they are angry they screech loudly. They have even been heard crying or whimpering when frightened. This has been observed in chicks about to leave the nest as well as in adult birds after the loss of a mate.

Tawnies are found in all parts of Australia and have clever ways of adapting to different climates. When it's hot, they produce a special kind of mucus in their mouths that cools the air as they breathe in. When it's cold, they go into torpor — a type of short-term hibernation where they slow their heart rate to conserve energy.

# VOGELKOP SUPERB BIRD-OF-PARADISE

## The dancing black crescent

**Location:** Tropical forests of West Papua, Indonesia

**Lifespan:** About 5–8 years

**Length:** About 25 cm

**Conservation status:** Least concern

The Vogelkop superb bird-of-paradise was only identified in 2018. It is similar in appearance to its closest relative, the better known greater superb bird-of-paradise, but it is just distinct enough to have been named a whole new species.

These birds look fairly normal most of the time, but when the males perform their courtship dance they transform into a very unusual shape. To prepare for his display, the male will clear his chosen branch of any dirt or stray leaves, and then let out a loud call to attract a female. When she arrives he kicks off the performance: he fans his wings behind his head, snaps open his bright breast feathers, throws back his head and opens his bright yellow mouth. His iridescent blue crown looks like two eyes staring out of his black feathers, which are some of the blackest feathers on earth.

The male's feathers absorb almost 100 per cent of the light that hits them, which is why they look completely black with little feather definition.

The Vogelkop male then shuffles from side to side around the female. His tiny fast steps make him appear as though he is gliding back and forth along the branch.

One reason Vogelkop males have developed such an elaborate courtship ritual is because the species has an unusually low population of females — and they are notoriously hard to impress.

# TUFTED COQUETTE

## The tiny jewel of the Amazon

**Location:** North-eastern regions of South America

**Weight:** 2-3 g

**Length:** 6-8 cm

**Conservation status:** Least concern

One of the smallest birds in the world, the tufted coquette is a tiny species of hummingbird from South America.

They feed primarily on nectar, which they lick from inside flowers using their long extendible tongues.

They are so tiny they could easily be confused with a large bee as they dart from flower to flower, wings beating so fast they look like a blur.

Like most hummingbirds, tufted coquettes are solitary creatures. They don't form flocks and only come together to breed. Males try to attract a female by flying in a u-shaped pattern in front of her, and, after mating has been successful, the male flies away again, leaving the female to raise the chicks alone.

The female tufted coquette chooses a nest site close to a good source of nectar. She then builds her small cup-shaped nest on a branch hidden about two metres above the ground.

The female usually lays two tiny eggs which are incubated for two weeks before hatching. Once they are hatched, she feeds her chicks a regurgitated mix of nectar and insects, using her beak to push the food right down their throats.

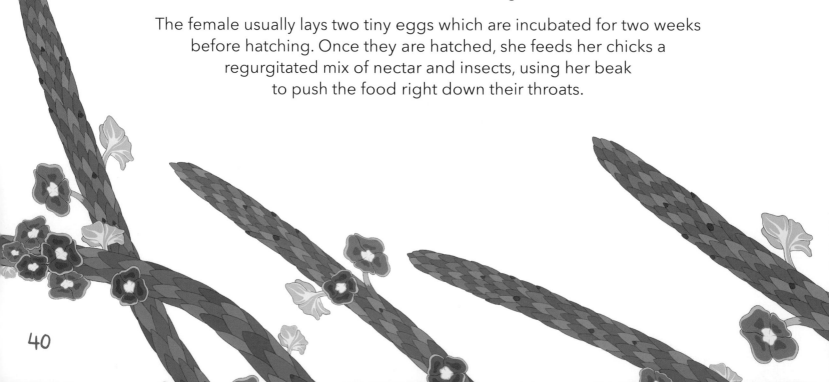

# GREATER SAGE-GROUSE

## The booming sage

**Location:** Sagebrush plains of western and central North America

**Wingspan:** 71-97 cm

**Height:** 48-76 cm

**Conservation status:** Near threatened

The greater sage-grouse is a large species of grouse that gets its name from its favourite food: sagebrush leaves. They are social birds that like to gather in large flocks. While they can fly, they much prefer to stay on their feet and generally only fly if they need to quickly escape danger.

Males and females look very different from each other. The females have a more subdued brown colouring, which helps them to stay well camouflaged while they are nesting.

The males have large inflatable chest sacs and striking white, black and yellow feathers, and are almost twice the size of the females.

Breeding season, when the males gather in leks, is an exciting time for greater sage-grouse. The males put on a bold display by strutting around with their tails fanned out, swishing their wings, and filling and emptying their large air sacs to make a popping or booming sound that can be heard up to a kilometre and a half away. A curious feature of this ritual is that the males will perform standing to the side of the females rather than in front of them. This is because the sound is louder, and therefore more impressive, from this position.

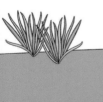
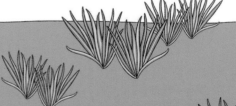

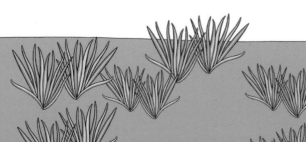

# TUFTED PUFFIN

## The fancy fish-catcher

**Location:** Islands and coastal areas of the northern Pacific
**Weight:** 520-1000 g

**Length:** Around 40 cm
**Conservation status:** Least concern

The tufted puffin is the largest puffin species. They have waterproof feathers and can drink salt water, meaning they can spend most of their time at sea, only coming to land during breeding season. Despite travelling far and wide across the water, puffins return to the place they were born each year to breed.

The colourful beaks and glossy yellow plumes these birds are famous for are only displayed during breeding time when both males and females put on a colourful show to help attract a mate. At the end of the season, they lose their plumes and their bills return to a dull reddish-brown colour.

Puffins form long-term pairs to breed and care for their young. They build a burrow together near the shore that can be up to two metres long, with a nesting chamber at the end. Each season, the female lays only one egg and both parents look after the chick, called a puffling, until it is ready to leave the nest at around six weeks old. The young puffling heads for the open sea, where it stays for two years before returning to the colony.

### Tufted puffins are powerful swimmers and can dive around 25 metres deep for up to a minute in the search of fish.

They have serrated bills to help them grip on to fish and they use their tongues to hold the fish against spiny grooves on the roof of their mouths while they catch more. A tufted puffin can hold ten or more fish crosswise in its bill at one time!

# GREAT GREY OWL

## The phantom of the north

**Location:** Northern regions of Europe, Asia and North America
**Wingspan:** About 1.5 m

**Length:** 61–84 cm
**Conservation status:** Least concern

Known as the phantom of the north for its silent and deadly hunting abilities, the great grey owl is the largest owl in the world. Male and female great grey owls look similar, but the female is even larger than the male.

Despite their size, great grey owls are not the heaviest owls — their fluffy feathers and long tails are deceptive.

The great grey owl's round facial discs are the largest of all birds of prey and are perfectly designed to aid hunting by directing sounds to its ears.

Like other owls, one ear is higher on its head than the other, but unusually they are not covered by tufts of feathers, which may be another reason why this owl's hearing is so sharp.

Great grey owls prefer small prey, and their diet is mostly made up of rodents, along with the occasional rabbit, squirrel, snake or small bird. They have the ability to 'snow plunge' on their prey — from their perch high up in the trees, great grey owls sit in silence, detecting the exact location of their prey with their sharp sense of hearing. They then plunge down into the snow with incredible accuracy, grasping their prey even if it is hiding under a metre of snow.

# GREATER PRAIRIE-CHICKEN

## The tunnel-digging chicken

**Location:** Plains and prairies of North America

**Wingspan:** About 70 cm

**Length:** About 43 cm

**Conservation status:** Near threatened

The greater prairie-chicken is actually a type of grouse. These striking birds live on the plains of North America, where they eat seeds, leaves and insects, and occasionally choose berries and young buds when they are available.

During winter thick snow covers the plains, but greater prairie-chickens are protected from the cold by the feathers on their legs and the tough skin on their feet.

## Sometimes they dig deep into the snow to make a tunnel that works like an igloo, staying out of the weather in the depths of winter.

In spring, male greater prairie-chickens will gather in a lek, inflate their bright yellow-orange air sacs, raise their tails and ear feathers, stamp their feet and occasionally leap into the air, all while letting out a loud, booming sound to attract a female.

The female is responsible for building a nest on the ground in areas of tall grass where her eggs will be hidden from predators. She usually lays up to 17 eggs and incubates them alone. Shortly after hatching, the chicks follow their mother away from the nest and are immediately responsible for finding their own food, although they do stay together for about three months.

# MAGNIFICENT FRIGATEBIRD

## The pirate of the Pacific

**Location:** The coast of the southern United States, Mexico and the Caribbean

**Wingspan:** Up to 2.3 m

**Length:** 89–114 cm

**Conservation status:** Least concern

The magnificent frigatebird does not have waterproof feathers, which is unusual for a seabird. This means it can't be in the water for more than a minute because its feathers will get waterlogged and it will be unable to take off again, so it will eventually drown. They also have short legs and small feet, meaning they can't paddle very well and are clumsy walkers. Luckily, they are extremely powerful flyers and spend most of their time in the air. In fact, they can fly for several days at a time without needing to land once!

Magnificent frigatebirds feed close to the shore on various fish, crustaceans, jellyfish and squid.

**They are notorious for stealing other birds' food and will swoop on another seabird mid-flight, grabbing it by its tail and shaking it until it regurgitates the fish it has just caught.**

The magnificent frigatebird then lets go and catches the regurgitated fish before it hits the water.

Nesting season sees the thievery continue, as magnificent frigatebirds like to steal sticks from other birds' nests to build their own. Magnificent frigatebirds breed throughout the year. Several males will surround one female, competing for her attention by inflating their large throat pouches and emitting high-pitched trills. When the female chooses a male, the pair perform an impressive acrobatic aerial display before the female completes her nest, using sticks brought to her by the male.

# WHITE-HEADED DUCK

## The master diver

**Location:** Lakes and wetlands of Asia, the Middle East, Europe and North Africa

**Wingspan:** 62–70 cm

**Length:** Around 43–48 cm

**Conservation status:** Endangered

The white-headed duck is a diving duck that doesn't like to fly. It spends much of its time diving repeatedly, staying completely underwater for five to seven seconds at a time, before surfacing for a gulp of air and diving again.

A social bird, white-headed ducks are not territorial and like to gather in large groups of around 500 birds, sometimes even thousands. Most white-headed ducks are migratory, moving across a large ranging habitat from Eastern Europe and the Middle East to Asia, according to the seasons, and food and breeding cycles. However, there are also populations of white-headed ducks in Spain and North Africa that don't migrate.

Males and females are around the same size but have quite different colourings, with the males' bright blue beaks making them stand out.

## Both males and females have a stiff tail that stands up vertically when they are floating on the water.

These ducks are a quiet species and are generally silent except during breeding season, when the males make a low rattling noise to attract a female. Female white-headed ducks build nests in vegetation over water, then lay the biggest egg relative to their size of any waterfowl (including swans and geese).

# VULTURINE GUINEA FOWL

## The brainy fowl

**Location:** Scrub, grasslands and arid areas of Central and East Africa

**Wingspan:** About 80 cm

**Length:** 60-72 cm

**Conservation status:** Least concern

The striking vulturine guinea fowl is so named because its bare head and neck look similar to a vulture. Yet from the neck down, they have some of the most beautifully coloured and patterned feathers in the bird kingdom.

Males and females look the same, but females are smaller. While vulturine guinea fowl are strong flyers, they much prefer to run – and, when threatened, will usually take off on foot. When they take to the air all together, however, the sound of their fast wing beats is so noisy most predators are put off by the sheer cacophony.

## Vulturine guinea fowl have a far more complex social structure than other birds, which indicates a uniquely high level of intelligence.

They live in groups for years at a time, and these groups choose to interact with other specific groups without any territorial aggression. Up to eight different groups have been observed roosting communally overnight, before separating again during the day. Vulturine guinea fowl appear to have social preferences for certain groups, suggesting they are not only able to keep track of individual birds within their own group but individuals in other groups as well. This type of behaviour has otherwise only been observed in large-brained mammals such as humans, apes, elephants and dolphins.

# WANDERING ALBATROSS

## The soaring world traveller

**Location:** Across the Southern Ocean

**Wingspan:** Up to 3.5 m

**Length:** Up to 1.35 m

**Conservation status:** Vulnerable

Wandering albatross live at sea and like to wander – they have been spotted across all the world's oceans, except the North Atlantic. They have the largest wingspan of any bird in the world. These expert gliders can fly for days or even weeks at a time, covering distances of over 900 kilometres a day without much effort and barely ever flapping their wings. They 'lock' their wings into a gliding posture so they don't have to waste energy holding them up, and then simply ride the wind – soaring and diving between currents of air in a pattern known as 'dynamic soaring'.

Wandering albatross feed on fish, squid and crustaceans by shallow diving into the ocean or eating from the surface of the water.

They have a bad habit of eating so much at once that they can't fly, and have to float on the water until they have properly digested their meal.

Wandering albatross always return to remote islands in the Southern Ocean to breed. Females lay a single large white egg, which is incubated by both parents. Albatross chicks grow very slowly, taking up to ten months to develop their flight feathers. When the chick finally flies out to sea, it stays away for five to ten years before it is ready to come back to land and mate.

With a long life of over 50 years and their wandering habits, wandering albatross are likely the most well-travelled animal on earth.

# GLOSSARY

| | |
|---|---|
| Aposematism | the use of bright colours, markings, sound or smell by an animal as a defence strategy or warning to discourage its predators |
| Casque | a helmet-like feature that some birds have on their heads or on top of their beaks |
| Endemic | only found in a particular place |
| Fledge | to leave the nest (after a chick has grown its flight feathers) |
| Lek | a gathering of male birds to perform a communal mating display in order to attract females; the site where such a performance takes place |
| Migratory | a type of animal that moves seasonally from one habitat to another in search of food and better conditions, or for breeding needs |
| Monogamous | the habit of having only one mate |
| Pollinator | a creature that carries pollen from one plant to another and aids the plant's fertilisation |
| Polygynous | the pattern of mating where males mate with several different females |
| Preen | to clean and groom feathers using the beak |
| Raptor | a bird of prey (a bird that feeds mainly or only on meat and that has a hooked beak and large sharp claws) |
| Roost | to settle down somewhere for rest or sleep |

The International Union for Conservation of Nature (IUCN) is the world's main authority on the conservation status of animal species. I have used classifications from the IUCN Red List of Threatened Species to describe the conservation status of each bird. The Red List classifies animals into nine categories using criteria such as population size, habitat range and rate of decline. The categories are:

| | |
|---|---|
| Extinct | No known individuals remaining |
| Extinct in the wild | Known only to survive in captivity or as a naturalised population outside its historic range |
| Critically endangered | Extremely high risk of extinction in the wild |
| Endangered | Very high risk of extinction in the wild |
| Vulnerable | High risk of extinction in the wild |
| Near threatened | Likely to become threatened in the near future |
| Least concern | Lowest risk; does not qualify for a more at-risk category |
| Data deficient | Not enough data to make an assessment |
| Not evaluated | Has not yet been evaluated against the criteria |

For more information go to www.iucnredlist.org

# ACKNOWLEDGEMENTS

This book has been in my mind for many years now and it's been such a joy to actually make it happen. As always, so many people behind the scenes have helped me bring this idea to life with their ideas and support.

Huge thanks to my publishing team at Hachette Australia, who always support me no matter how crazy my ideas are and how late my first drafts are! I couldn't ask for a better bunch of people to work with. Particular thanks to my editor Rebecca who meticulously goes through every letter and every stroke of the pen – my books are always better for your input and I'm extremely grateful to be working with you.

To my Red Parka Family – 2020/21 has been a challenge and for much of it I've been off-grid drawing feathers! Tracy, Charles, Lisa, Tess, Scarlett, Al, Jasper, Bronte and Fraser – thank you all for keeping the lights on at Red Parka through difficult circumstances, especially when I haven't been able to do it myself. And to the Red Parka extended family (that's you!) – thanks for buying my books and supporting my small business this year. More than ever we've needed your support, and we are grateful to every single one of you!

Final thanks go to my family – Gail, Sandy, Jo, Charles, Fraser, Cameron – for your love and support (and fact-checking and dinner-making). I'm immensely grateful for you all. And the biggest thanks of all to Tracy and Tess, my amazing wife and daughter – you two make my world go round and I love you more than all the curious birds in the whole world!

## ABOUT THE AUTHOR

Jennifer Cossins is a CBCA award-winning artist and writer with a passion for nature, the animal kingdom and all things bright and colourful. A born and bred Tasmanian, Jennifer also designs homewares, textiles and stationery, which she stocks in her store in Hobart, Red Parka. Jennifer's other books include *A–Z of Endangered Animals*, *101 Collective Nouns*, *The Baby Animal Book*, *A–Z of Australian Animals*, *The Ultimate Animal Counting Book*, *A Flamboyance of Flamingos*, *The Mummy Animal Book*, *The Daddy Animal Book* and *The Ultimate Animal Alphabet Book*.